<u>INDEX</u>

Once upon a time: Zarqawi

On a cold and blustery evening in December 1989, Huthaifa Azzam, the teenage son of the legendary Jordanian-Palestinian mujahideen leader Sheikh Abdullah Azzam, went to the airport in Peshawar, Pakistan, to welcome a group of young men. All were new recruits, largely from Jordan, and they had come to fight in a fratricidal civil war in neighboring Afghanistan—an outgrowth of the CIA-financed jihad of the 1980s against the Soviet occupation there.

The men were scruffy, Huthaifa mused as he greeted them, and seemed hardly in battle-ready form. Some had just been released from prison; others were professors and sheikhs. None of them would prove worth remembering—except for a relatively short, squat man named Ahmad Fadhil Nazzal al-Khalaylah. He would later rename himself Abu Musab al-Zarqawi.

Once one of the most wanted men in the world, for whose arrest the United States offered a $25 million reward, al-Zarqawi was a notoriously enigmatic figure—a man who was everywhere yet nowhere.

Huthaifa Azzam bridges both worlds. He first went into battle at the age of fifteen, fighting against the Soviets in Afghanistan with his father and Osama bin Laden (to whom his father was a spiritual mentor); three years later, on that December night at the Peshawar airport, he met al-Zarqawi for the first time. The two Azzams and bin Laden had fought against the Soviets in the early days of the jihad; al-Zarqawi would fight in the war's second phase, after the Soviets had pulled out. Both Huthaifa Azzam and al-Zarqawi would eventually leave Afghanistan to pursue two very different lives, but their paths would once again cross on the battlefields of jihad in Iraq, after the U.S. invasion of 2003.

A self-described jihadist—one who believes in struggle, or, more loosely, holy war—Azzam now lives in the Jordanian capital, Amman, where he is at work on a doctorate in classical Arabic literature, but he moves routinely between Jordan and Iraq.

Abu Musab al-Zarqawi, barely forty and barely literate, a Bedouin from the Bani Hassan tribe, was until recently almost unknown outside his native Jordan. Then, on February 5, 2003, Secretary of State Colin Powell catapulted him onto the world stage. In his address to the United Nations making the case for war in Iraq, Powell identified al-Zarqawi—mistakenly, as it turned out—as the crucial link between al-Qaeda and Saddam Hussein's regime. Subsequently, al-Zarqawi became a leading figure in the insurgency in Iraq—and in November of last year, he also brought his jihadist revolution back home, as the architect of three lethal hotel bombings in Amman.

His notoriety grew with every atrocity he perpetrated, yet Western and Middle Eastern intelligence officials remained bedeviled by a simple question: Who was he? Was he al-Qaeda's point man in Iraq, as the Bush administration argued repeatedly? Or was he, as a retired Israeli intelligence official told not long ago, a staunch rival of bin Laden's, whose importance the United States exaggerated in order to validate a link between al-Qaeda and pre-war Iraq, and to put a non-Iraqi face on a complex insurgency?

Bin Laden and Zarqawi had little in common: bin Laden, like most of his inner circle, is a university graduate from an influential family; al-Zarqawi, like many who follow him, was from an anonymous family (even though they are members of a significant tribe) and an anonymous town—a man who was fired from a job as a video-store clerk and whose background included street gangs and, according to Jordanian intelligence officials, prison for sexual assault. He was a ruthless self-promoter who, U.S. officials claim, killed or wounded thousands of people in three years (2003-2006)—in suicide bombings, mass executions, and beheadings that have been videotaped. He developed a mythic aura of invulnerability. But he was not the terrorist mastermind that he was often claimed to be.

Zarqa is a shambolic industrial city of some 850,000 people, a sprawl of factories, open fields, and dust. Twenty-five miles northeast of Amman, it is Jordan's third-largest city, and one of its most militant. For years it has been a magnet for Islamic activists. Along with the cities of Irbid and Salt, it has sent the largest number of Jordanian volunteers to fight abroad, first in Afghanistan and now in Iraq. Al-Zarqawi was born and raised in the al-Masoum neighborhood of Zarqa's old city, which sprawls somewhat haphazardly into the al-Ruseifah Palestinian refugee camp. (*More than 60 percent of Jordan's 5.9 million inhabitants are Palestinian, as are some 80 percent of the inhabitants of old Zarqa.*)

Until his death, al-Zarqawi kept a home on a quiet lane in Zarqa. It was indistinguishable from its neighbors—a two-story white stucco building surrounded by a whitewashed wall. The house was empty,; al-Zarqawi's sisters, who still live in Zarqa, would come by to look after it.

The first of al-Zarqawi's two wives had lived in the house until recently. She was his cousin, whom he had married when he was twenty-two. They had four children, two boys and two girls. But not long before my visit, al-Zarqawi had sent an unknown man to drive them across the border to be with him in Iraq. His second wife, a Jordanian-Palestinian whom he had married in Afghanistan, and with whom he has a son, was reported to be with him in Iraq as well. Al-Zarqawi's mother, Omm Sayel, whom he adored—and who had traveled to Peshawar with him when he joined the jihad—died of leukemia in 2004; although he was the most wanted man in Jordan at the time of her death, al-Zarqawi returned to Zarqa in disguise to attend her funeral.

Afganistan

Al-Zarqawi was based initially in the border town of Khost, which, after both the Americans and the Soviets had left Afghanistan, was the site of intense and heavily contested battles between the mujahideen and the pro-Soviet Najibullah regime. At the beginning, al-Zarqawi had not been a fighter but had tried his hand at being a journalist. He had worked as a reporter for a small jihadist magazine, *Al-Bonian al Marsous*.

"*He was an ordinary guy, an ordinary fighter, and didn't really distinguish himself,*" Huthaifa Azzam said of al-Zarqawi's first time in Afghanistan. "*He was a quiet guy who didn't talk much. But he was brave. Zarqawi doesn't know the meaning of fear. He's been wounded five or six times in Afghanistan and Iraq. He seems to intentionally place himself in the middle of the most dangerous situations. He fought in the battles of Khost and Kardez and, in April 1992, witnessed the liberation of Kabul by the mujahideen. A lot of Arabs were great commanders during those years. Zarqawi was not. He also wasn't very religious during that time. In fact, he'd only 'returned' to Islam three months before coming to Afghanistan. It was the Tablighi Jamaat [a proselytizing missionary* group spread across the Muslim world] *who convinced him—he had thirty-seven criminal cases against him by then—that it was time to cleanse himself."*

His second time in Afghanistan was far more important than the first. But the first was significant in two ways. Zarqawi was young and impressionable; he'd never been out of Jordan before, and now, for the first time, he was interacting with doctrinaire Islamists from across the Muslim world, most of them brought to Afghanistan by the CIA. It was also his first exposure to al-Qaeda. He didn't meet bin Laden, of course, but he trained in one of his and Abdullah Azzam's camps: the Sada camp near the Afghan border inside Pakistan. He trained under Abu Hafs al-Masri." (*The reference was to the nom de guerre of Mohammed Atef, an Egyptian who was bin Laden's military chief and, until he was killed in an American air strike in Afghanistan in November 2001, the No. 3 official in al-Qaeda.*)

Abu Muntassir Bilah Muhammad is another jihadist who spent time fighting in Afghanistan and who would later become one of the co-founders of al-Zarqawi's first militant Islamist group. *"Zarqawi arrived in Afghanistan as a zero, a man with no career, just floundering about. He trained and fought and he came back to Jordan with ambitions and dreams: to carry the ideology of jihad. His first ambition was to reform Jordan, to set up an Islamist state. And there was a cachet involved in fighting in the jihad. Zarqawi returned to Jordan with newfound respect. It's not so much what Zarqawi did in the jihad—it's what the jihad did for him."*

With an eye to the future, al-Zarqawi also used the jihad years to begin the process of cultivating friendships that would eventually lead to the formation of an international support network for his activities. Particularly when he was in Khost, his primary friendships were with the Saudi fighters and others from the Gulf. Some of them were millionaires. There were even a couple of billionaires.

But perhaps as important as anything else, it was in Afghanistan that al-Zarqawi was introduced to Sheikh Abu Muhammad al-Maqdisi (*whose real name is Isam Muhammad Tahir al-Barqawi*), a revered and militant Salafist cleric who had moved to Zarqa following the mass expulsion of Palestinians from Kuwait in the aftermath of the Gulf War. The Salafiya movement originated in Egypt, at the end of the nineteenth century, as a modernist Sunni reform movement, the aim of which was to let the Muslim world rise to the challenges posed by Western science and political thought. But since the 1920s, it has evolved into a severely puritanical school of absolutist thought that is markedly anti-Western and based on a literal interpretation of the Koran.

Today's most radical Salafists regard any departure from their own rigid principles of Islam to be heretical; their particular hatred of Shiites—who broke with the Sunnis in 632 A.D. over the question of succession to the Prophet Muhammad, and who now constitute the majority in Iran and Iraq—is visceral. Over the years, al-Maqdisi embraced the most extreme school of Salafism, closely akin to the puritanical Wahhabism of Saudi Arabia, and in the early 1980s he published *The Creed of Abraham*, the single most important source of teachings for Salafist movements around the world.

Al-Zarqawi and al-Maqdisi left Afghanistan in 1993 and returned to Jordan. They found it much changed. In their absence the Jordanians and the Israelis had begun negotiations that would lead to the signing of a peace treaty in 1994; the Palestinians had signed the Oslo Accords of 1993; and the Iraqis had lost the Gulf War. Unemployment was up sharply, the result of a privatization drive agreed to with the International Monetary Fund, and Jordanians were frustrated and angry. The Muslim Brotherhood—the kingdom's only viable opposition political force, which had agreed to support King Hussein in exchange for being allowed to participate in public and parliamentary life—appeared unable to cope with the rising disaffection. Small underground Islamist groups had therefore begun to appear, composed largely of men who had fought in the Afghan jihad, and who were guided by the increasingly loud voices of militant clerics who felt the Muslim Brotherhood had been co-opted by the state.

After the two men returned home, al-Maqdisi toured the kingdom, preaching and recruiting, and al-Zarqawi sought out Abu Muntassir, who had already acquired a standing among Islamic militants in Jordan. Despite their enthusiasm, al-Zarqawi, al-Maqdisi, and Abu Muntassir did not appear to be natural revolutionaries. Their first operation was in Zarqa, in 1993, when al-Zarqawi dispatched one of their men to a local cinema with orders to blow it up because it was showing pornographic films. But the hapless would-be bomber apparently got so distracted by what was happening on the screen that he forgot about his bomb. It exploded and blew off his legs.

In another botched operation, al-Maqdisi (according to court testimony that he denied) gave al-Zarqawi seven grenades he had smuggled into Jordan, and al-Zarqawi hid them in the cellar of his family's home. Al-Maqdisi was already under surveillance by Jordan's intelligence service by that time, because of his growing popularity. The grenades were quickly discovered, and the two men, along with a number of their followers, found themselves for the first time before a state security court. Al-Zarqawi told the court that he had found the grenades while walking down the street. The judges were not amused. They convicted him and al-Maqdisi of possessing illegal weapons and belonging to a banned organization. In 1994, al-Zarqawi was sentenced to fifteen years in prison. He would flourish there.

Al-Zarqawi embraced prison life in the extreme—as he appears to have embraced everything. According to fellow inmates of his, his primary obsessions were recruiting other prisoners to his cause, building his body, and, under the tutelage of al-Maqdisi, memorizing the 6,236 verses of the Koran. He was stern, tough, and unrelenting on anything that he considered to be an infraction of his rules, yet he was often seen in the prison courtyard crying as he read the Koran.

He was fastidious about his appearance in prison—his beard and moustache were always cosmetically groomed—and he wore only Afghan dress: the *shalwar kameez* and a rolled-brim, woolen Pashtun cap. Islamists flocked to him. He attracted recruits; some joined him out of fascination, others out of curiosity, and still others out of fear. In a short time, he had organized prison life at Swaqa like a gang leader.

There were also confrontations and altercations with prison officials and guards. Whether al-Zarqawi was ever tortured is a matter of dispute: some of his followers say he was; Jordanian government officials, perhaps predictably, say he was not.

Al-Zarqawi controlled not only his followers but also the ward's television sets. No one could really *watch* them, however, since he had covered them with black cloth to prevent the display of female forms. All the inmates could do was listen—and only to the evening news at eight o'clock.

Al-Zarqawi and al-Maqdisi's Bayat al-Imam continued to grow, both inside prison and in Zarqa, Irbid, and Salt. Al-Zarqawi used his Bedouin credentials to good effect, as his own profile began to ascend. His Bani Hassan tribe is one of the Middle East's most prominent, and its tribal lands spill across the borders dividing Jordan, Syria, and Iraq. In Jordan, many of its members hold high-level positions in the government, the army, and the intelligence service. As a result, many of the prisoners, and many of Swaqa's guards, deferred to al-Zarqawi. Al-Maqdisi, a Palestinian, was also accorded special treatment, but largely as a result of his links to al-Zarqawi and the Bani Hassan. Between mentor and pupil, the roles had subtly begun to shift inside the prison walls.

As al-Zarqawi recruited, al-Maqdisi preached, and using the Internet, they broadcast their message of jihad across three continents. Sheikh Abu Qatada, a Palestinian cleric who is one of Salafism's leading ideologues, was also one of al-Maqdisi's closest friends. The two men had been together in Kuwait, then in Zarqa, then Afghanistan. Abu Qatada, after leaving Afghanistan, had moved to London (where he is currently under arrest, awaiting possible deportation to Jordan). Now al-Maqdisi's religious tracts were smuggled out of Swaqa by prisoners' wives and mothers, with help from sympathetic prison guards, and they were sent on to Abu Qatada, who posted them on the Web sites of Salafists and jihadists throughout Europe, the Middle East, and the Persian Gulf.

Al-Zarqawi's own religious views became increasingly severe, as did his intolerance of anyone he believed to be an infidel. Al-Maqdisi sometimes angrily disagreed with him. It was the first portent of what lay ahead. Al-Zarqawi began to eclipse his mentor in prison, and would continue to do so over the coming years, but their final, and public, break did not occur until November 2005, when, on Al-Jazeera, al-Maqdisi criticized his former protégé for the hotel bombings in Amman. Nevertheless, despite their prison disagreements, al-Maqdisi, from time to time, permitted al-Zarqawi to draft his own religious tracts. Abu Muntassir who would also later break with al-Zarqawi was his editor.

In May of the following year (1999), Jordan's King Abdullah II—newly enthroned after the death of his father, King Hussein—declared a general amnesty, and al-Zarqawi was released from Swaqa. He had made effective use of his time there. As he had done nearly a decade before—when he befriended wealthy Saudi jihadists in Khost—he had expanded his reach and his appeal during his prison years. Among the fellow inmates he had converted to Salafism and brought into the Bayat al-Imam were a substantial number of prisoners from Iraq.

After returning for a few months to Zarqa, al-Zarqawi left again and traveled to Pakistan. He may or may not have known that Jordan was about to declare him a suspect in a series of foiled terrorist attacks intended for New Year's Eve of

1999. The plan, which became known as the "Millennium Plot," involved the bombing of Christian landmarks and other tourist sites, along with the Radisson Hotel in Amman. Had it succeeded, it would have been al-Zarqawi's first involvement in a major terrorist attack.

Whatever the case, al-Zarqawi planned ahead before he left for Pakistan. He arrived bearing a letter of introduction from Abu Kutaiba al-Urduni, one of Jordan's most significant leaders during the jihad in Afghanistan. Al-Urduni had been a key deputy to—and the chief recruiter inside Jordan for—Sheikh Abdullah Azzam, Huthaifa Azzam's father. Having worked for years in Peshawar as the leader of the Service Office, or the Maktab al-Khidmat, the sheikh had become *the* pivotal figure in the Pan-Islamic recruitment of volunteers for the jihad.) Al-Urduni's letter was the first endorsement that al-Zarqawi had received from such a senior figure—and the letter was addressed to Osama bin Laden.

In December 1999, al-Zarqawi crossed the border into Afghanistan, and later that month he and bin Laden met at the Government Guest House in the southern city of Kandahar, the de facto capital of the ruling Taliban. According to several different accounts of the meeting, bin Laden distrusted and disliked al-Zarqawi immediately. He suspected that the group of Jordanian prisoners with whom al-Zarqawi had been granted amnesty earlier in the year had been infiltrated by Jordanian intelligence.

Something similar had occurred not long before with a Jordanian jihadist cell that had come to Afghanistan. Bin Laden also disliked al-Zarqawi's swagger and the green tattoos on his left hand, which he reportedly considered un-Islamic. Al-Zarqawi came across to bin Laden as aggressively ambitious, abrasive, and overbearing. His hatred of Shiites also seemed to bin Laden to be potentially divisive—which, of course, it was. Bin Laden's mother, to whom he remains close, is a Shiite, from the Alawites of Syria.

Al-Zarqawi would not recant, even in the presence of the legendary head of al-Qaeda. "Shiites should be executed," he reportedly declared. He also took exception to bin Laden's providing Arab fighters to the Taliban, the fundamentalist student militia that, although now in power, was still battling the Northern Alliance, which controlled some 10 percent of Afghanistan. Muslim killing Muslim was un-Islamic, al-Zarqawi is reported to have said. Unaccustomed to such direct criticism, the leader of al-Qaeda was aghast.

A former Egyptian army colonel who had trained in special operations, al-Adel was then al-Qaeda's chief of security and a prominent voice in an emerging debate gripping the militant Islamist world. Who should the primary target be—the "near enemy" (the Muslim world's "un-Islamic" regimes) or the "far enemy" (primarily Israel and the United States)? Al-Zarqawi was a near-enemy advocate, and although his obsession remained the overthrow of the Jordanian monarchy, he had expanded his horizons slightly during his prison years and had now begun to focus on the area known as al-Sham, or the Levant, which includes Jordan, Syria, Lebanon, and historic Palestine.

As an Egyptian who had attempted to overthrow his own country's army-backed regime, al-Adel saw merit in al-Zarqawi's views. Thus, after a good deal of debate within al-Qaeda, it was agreed that al-Zarqawi would be given $5,000 or so in "seed money" to set up his own training camp outside the western Afghan city of Herat, near the Iranian border. It was about as far away as he could be from bin Laden. Saif al-Adel was designated the middleman.

In early 2000, with a dozen or so followers who had arrived from Peshawar and Amman, al-Zarqawi set out for the western desert encircling Herat. His goal: to build an army that he could export to anywhere in the world. Al-Adel paid monthly visits to al-Zarqawi's training camp; later, on his Web site, he would write that he was amazed at what he saw there. The number of al-Zarqawi's fighters multiplied from dozens to hundreds during the following year, and by the time the forces evacuated their camp, prior to the U.S. air strikes of October 2001, the fighters and their families numbered some 2,000 to 3,000. According to al-Adel, the wives of al-Zarqawi's followers served lavish Levantine cuisine in the camp.

It was in Herat that al-Zarqawi formed the militant organization Jund al-Sham, or Soldiers of the Levant. His key operational lieutenants were mainly Syrians—most of whom had fought in the Afghan jihad, and many of whom belonged to their country's banned Muslim Brotherhood. The Brotherhood's exiled leadership, which is largely based in Europe, was immensely important in recruiting for the Herat camp, although whether it also supplied funds remains under debate. What is clear, however, is that al-Zarqawi's closest aide, a Syrian from the city of Hama named Sulayman Khalid Darwish—or Abu al-Ghadiyah—was considered to be, one of al-Zarqawi's most likely successors.

For Zarqawi, it was the turning point. Herat was the beginning of what he is now. He had command responsibilities for the first time; he had a battle plan.

And even though he and bin Laden never got on, he was important to them. Herat was the only training camp in Afghanistan that was actively recruiting volunteers specifically from the Sham. In Herat, he called himself the 'Emir of Sham'!"

At least five times, in 2000 and 2001, bin Laden called al-Zarqawi to come to Kandahar and pay *bayat*—take an oath of allegiance—to him. Each time, al-Zarqawi refused. Under no circumstances did he want to become involved in the battle between the Northern Alliance and the Taliban. He also did not believe that either bin Laden or the Taliban was serious enough about jihad.

When the United States launched its air war inside Afghanistan, on October 7, 2001, al-Zarqawi joined forces with al-Qaeda and the Taliban for the first time. He and his Jund al-Sham fought in and around Herat and Kandahar. Al-Zarqawi was wounded in an American air strike—not in the leg, as U.S. officials claimed for two years, but in the chest, when the ceiling of the building in which he was operating collapsed on him. Neither did he join Osama bin Laden in the eastern mountains of Tora Bora, as U.S. officials have also said. Bin Laden took only his most trusted fighters to Tora Bora, and al-Zarqawi was not one of them.

In December 2001, accompanied by some 300 fighters from Jund al-Sham, al-Zarqawi left Afghanistan once again, and entered Iran.

During the next fourteen months, al-Zarqawi based himself primarily in Iran and in the autonomous area of Kurdistan, in northern Iraq, traveling from time to time to Syria and to the Ayn al-Hilwah Palestinian refugee camp in the south of Lebanon—a camp that became his main recruiting ground. More often, however, al-Zarqawi traveled to the Sunni Triangle of Iraq. He expanded his network, recruited and trained new fighters, and set up bases, safe houses, and military training camps. In Iran, he was reunited with Saif al-Adel—who encouraged him to go to Iraq and provided contacts there—and for a time, al-Zarqawi stayed at a farm belonging to the fiercely anti-American Afghan jihad leader Gulbaddin Hekmatyar. In Kurdistan he lived and worked with the separatist militant Islamist group Ansar al-Islam, ironically in an area protected as part of the "no-fly" zone imposed on Saddam Hussein by Washington.

One can only imagine how astonished al-Zarqawi must have been when Colin Powell named him as the crucial link between al-Qaeda and Saddam Hussein's regime. He was not even officially a part of al-Qaeda, and ever since he had left Afghanistan, his links had been not to Iraq but to Iran.

In the beginning the Iranians gave him automatic weapons, uniforms, military equipment, when he was with the army of Ansar al-Islam. Now they essentially just turn a blind eye to his activities, and to those of al-Qaeda generally. The Iranians see Iraq as a fight against the Americans, and overall, they'll get rid of Zarqawi and all of his people once the Americans are out.

In the summer of 2003, three months after the American invasion, al-Zarqawi moved to the Sunni areas of Iraq. He became infamous almost at once. On August 7, he allegedly carried out a car-bomb attack at the Jordanian embassy in Baghdad. Twelve days later, he was linked to the bombing of the United Nations headquarters, in which twenty-two people died. And on August 29, in what was then the deadliest attack of the war, he engineered the killing of over a hundred people, including a revered cleric, the Ayatollah Muhammad Baqr al-Hakim, in a car bombing outside Shia Islam's holy shrine in Najaf. The suicide bomber in that attack was Yassin Jarad, from Zarqa. He was al-Zarqawi's father-in-law.

Even then—and even more so now—Zarqawi was not the main force in the insurgency. To establish himself, he carried out the Muhammad Hakim operation, and the attack against the UN. Both of them gained a lot of support for him—with the tribes, with Saddam's army and other remnants of his regime. They made Zarqawi the *symbol* of the resistance in Iraq, but not the leader. And he never has been."

The Americans have been patently stupid in all of this. They've blown Zarqawi so out of proportion that, of course, his prestige has grown. And as a result, sleeper cells from all over Europe are coming to join him now.

Of course, no one did more to cultivate that image than al-Zarqawi himself. He committed some of the deadliest attacks in Iraq, though they still represent only some 10 percent of the country's total number of attacks. In May 2004, he inaugurated his notorious wave of hostage beheadings; he also specialized in suicide and truck bombings of Shiite shrines and mosques, largely in Shiite neighborhoods. His primary aim was to provoke a civil war. *"If we succeed in dragging [the Shia] into a sectarian war,"* he purportedly wrote in a letter intercepted by U.S. forces and released in February 2004, *"this will awaken the sleepy Sunnis who are fearful of destruction and death at the hands of the Shia."*

Al-Zarqawi courted chaos so that Iraq would provide him another failed state to operate in after the overthrow of the Taliban in Afghanistan. He became best known for his videotaped beheadings. One after the other they appeared on jihadist Web sites, always the same. In the background was the trademark black banner of al-Zarqawi's newest group: al-Tawhid wa al-Jihad, or Monotheism and Jihad. In the foreground, a blindfolded hostage, kneeling and pleading for his life, was dressed in an orange jumpsuit resembling those worn by the detainees at Guantánamo Bay.

Al-Zarqawi's first victim was a Pennsylvania engineer named Nicholas Berg. In the video, five hooded men, dressed in black, stand behind Berg. After a recitation, one of the men pulls a long knife from his shirt, steps forward, and slices off Berg's head. The U.S. military quickly announced that the executioner was al-Zarqawi himself, and although no one doubts that he planned the operation, questions soon arose: the figure seems taller than al-Zarqawi, and he uses his right hand to wield the knife. Al-Zarqawi was said to be left-handed.

Regardless of his growing notoriety in Iraq, al-Zarqawi never lost sight of his ultimate goal: the overthrow of the Jordanian monarchy. His efforts to foment unrest in Jordan included the 2002 assassination of the U.S. diplomat Lawrence Foley, and, on a far larger scale, a disrupted plot in 2004 to bomb the headquarters of the Jordanian intelligence services—a scheme that, according to Jordanian officials, would have entailed the use of trucks packed with enough chemicals and explosives to kill some 80,000 people. Once it was uncovered, al-Zarqawi immediately accepted responsibility for the plot, although he denied that chemical weapons would have been involved.

Later that year, in October 2004, after resisting for nearly five years, al-Zarqawi finally paid *bayat* to Osama bin Laden—but only after eight months of often stormy negotiations. After doing so he proclaimed himself to be the "Emir of al-Qaeda's Operations in the Land of Mesopotamia," a title that subordinated him to bin Laden but at the same time placed him firmly on the global stage.

One explanation for this coming together of these two former antagonists was simple: al-Zarqawi profited from the al-Qaeda franchise, and bin Laden needed a presence in Iraq. Another explanation is more complex: bin Laden laid claim to al-Zarqawi in the hopes of forestalling his emergence as the single most important terrorist figure in the world, and al-Zarqawi accepted bin Laden's endorsement to augment his credibility and to strengthen his grip on the Iraqi tribes. Both explanations are true. It was a pragmatic alliance, but tenuous from the start.

The attacks, which represented an expansion of al- Zarqawi's sophistication and reach, also showed his growing independence from the al-Qaeda chief. They came only thirteen months after he had sworn *bayat*. The alliance had already begun to fray.

The signs were visible as early as the summer of 2005. In a letter purportedly sent to al-Zarqawi in July from Ayman al-Zawahiri, the Egyptian surgeon who is bin Laden's designated heir, al-Zarqawi was chided about his tactics in Iraq. And although some experts have cast doubt on the letter's authenticity (it was released by the office of the U.S. Director of National Intelligence), few would dispute its message: namely, that al-Zarqawi's hostage beheadings, his mass slaughter of Shiites, and his assaults on their mosques were all having a negative effect on Muslim opinion—both of him and, by extension, of al-Qaeda—around the world. In one admonition, al-Zawahiri allegedly advised al-Zarqawi that a captive can be killed as easily by a bullet as by a knife.

Then, in early April, Huthaifa Azzam announced that the "Iraqi resistance's high command" had stripped al-Zarqawi of his political role and relegated him to military operations. It was the second time that al-Zarqawi's profile had seemingly been lowered—or that he had lowered it—this year. The first had come in January, when it was announced that al-Qaeda in Iraq had joined five other Sunni insurgent groups to form a coalition called the Mujahideen Shura Council. By early May, U.S. counterterrorism analysts were still puzzling over what the two events meant and what changes they could portend.

As they debated, al-Zarqawi sprang to life again, in a video posted on the Internet on April 24. It was the first time he had appeared in a jihadist videotape, and the first time he had shown his face. Dressed in black fatigues and a black cap, he had ammunition pouches strapped across his chest. He appeared fit, if overweight, as he posed in the desert firing an automatic weapon and as he sat with a group of masked aides, apparently plotting strategy. It seemed an extremely risky thing for him to do, and yet it also appeared to be very deliberate. It was a useful tool for recruitment, intending to show al-Zarqawi as both a flamboyant fighter and a pensive strategist. More important than anything else, however, it was meant to show the world that

Abu Musab al-Zarqawi—the brash young man who had come of age in the rough-and-tumble of Zarqa—remained relevant.

Back to the Future

Military action is necessary to halt the spread of the ISIS "cancer," said President Obama. In his much anticipated address, he called for expanded airstrikes across Iraq and Syria, and new measures to arm and train Iraqi and Kurdish ground forces.

Missing from the chorus of outrage, however, has been any acknowledgement of the integral role of covert US and British regional military intelligence strategy in empowering and even directly sponsoring the very same virulent Islamist militants in Iraq, Syria and beyond, that went on to break away from al-Qaeda and form 'ISIS', the Islamic State of Iraq and Syria, or now simply, the Islamic State (IS).

Since 2003, Anglo-American power has secretly and openly coordinated direct and indirect support for Islamist terrorist groups linked to al-Qaeda across the Middle East and North Africa. This ill-conceived patchwork geo-strategy is a legacy of the persistent influence of neoconservative ideology, motivated by longstanding but often contradictory ambitions to dominate regional oil resources, defend an expansionist Israel, and in pursuit of these, re-draw the map of the Middle East.

Now despite Pentagon denials that there will be boots on the ground – and Obama's insistence that this would not be another "Iraq war" – local Kurdish military and intelligence sources confirm that US and German special operations forces are already "on the ground" here. US airstrikes on ISIS positions and arms supplies to the Kurds have also been accompanied by British RAF reconnaissance flights over the region and UK weapons shipments to Kurdish peshmerga forces.

Early during the 2003 invasion and occupation of Iraq, the US covertly supplied arms to al-Qaeda affiliated insurgents even while ostensibly supporting an emerging Shi'a-dominated administration.

Pakistani defense sources interviewed by Asia Times in February 2005 confirmed that insurgents described as "former Ba'ath party" loyalists – who were being recruited and trained by "al-Qaeda in Iraq" under the leadership of the late Abu Musab Zarqawi – were being supplied Pakistan-manufactured weapons by the US. The arms shipments included rifles, rocket-propelled grenade launchers, ammunition, rockets and other light weaponry.

These arms *"could not be destined for the Iraqi security forces because US arms would be given to them"*, a source told Syed Saleem Shahzad – the Times' Pakistan bureau chief who, "known for his exposes of the Pakistani military" according to the New Yorker, was murdered in 2011. Rather, the US is playing a double-game to "head off" the threat of a "Shi'ite clergy-driven religious movement," said the Pakistani defense source. This was not the only way US strategy aided the rise of Zarqawi, a bin Laden mentee and brainchild of the extremist ideology that would later spawn 'ISIS.'

Dividing Enemies

According to a little-known report *"Dividing Our Enemies"*, made by US Joint Special Operations University (JSOU), post-invasion Iraq was an interesting case study of fanning discontent among enemies, leading to 'red-against-red' [enemy-against-enemy] firefights. While counter-insurgency on the one hand requires US forces to ameliorate harsh or deprived living conditions of the indigenous populations to publicly win local hearts and minds.

In other words, US forces would pursue public legitimacy through conventional social welfare while simultaneously de-legitimizing local enemies by escalating intra-insurgent violence, knowing full-well that doing so will in turn escalate the number of innocent civilians *"caught in the crossfire."* The idea is that violence covertly calibrated by US special operations will not only weaken enemies through in-fighting but turn the population against them.

In this case, the 'enemy' consisted of jihadists, Ba'athists, and peaceful Sufis, who were in a majority but, like the militants, also opposed the US military presence and therefore needed to be influenced. The JSOU report referred to events in late 2004 in Fallujah where *"US psychological warfare (PSYOP) specialists"* undertook to *"set insurgents battling insurgents."*

This involved actually promoting Zarqawi's ideology, ironically, to defeat it: *"The PSYOP warriors crafted programs to exploit Zarqawi's murderous activities – and to disseminate them through meetings, radio and television broadcasts, handouts, newspaper stories, political cartoons, and posters – thereby diminishing his folk-hero image,"* and encouraging the different factions to pick each other off. *"By tapping into the Fallujans' revulsion and antagonism to the*

Zarqawi jihadis the Joint PSYOP Task Force did its 'best to foster a rift between Sunni groups.'"

Yet as noted by Dahr Jamail, one of the few unembedded investigative reporters in Iraq after the war, the proliferation of propaganda linking the acceleration of suicide bombings to the persona of Zarqawi was not matched by meaningful evidence. His own search to substantiate the myriad claims attributing the insurgency to Zarqawi beyond anonymous US intelligence sources encountered only an *"eerie blankness"*.

The US military operation in Fallujah, largely justified on the claim that Zarqawi's militant forces had occupied the city, used white phosphorous, cluster bombs, and indiscriminate air strikes to pulverize 36,000 of Fallujah's 50,000 homes, killing nearly a thousand civilians, terrorizing 300,000 inhabitants to flee, and culminating in a disproportionate increase in birth defects, cancer and infant mortality due to the devastating environmental consequences of the war.

To this day, Fallujah has suffered from being largely cut-off from wider Iraq, its infrastructure largely unworkable with water and sewage systems still in disrepair, and its citizens subject to sectarian discrimination and persecution by Iraqi government backed Shi'a militia and police. *"Thousands of bereaved and homeless Falluja families have a new reason to hate the US and its allies,"* observed The Guardian in 2005. Thus, did the US occupation plant the seeds from which Zarqawi's legacy would coalesce into the Frankenstein monster that calls itself "the Islamic State."

Camp Bucca

Beyond conspiracy theories – which are often justified in an era where everything appears as though it is part of a plan or a scheme – we have the right to ask why the majority of the leaders of the Islamic State (IS), formerly the Islamic State in Iraq and Syria (ISIS), had all been incarcerated in the same prison at Camp Bucca, which was run by the US occupation forces near Omm Qasr in southeastern Iraq.

In the context of conspiracy theories, there are a lot of rumors about links between IS and the US intelligence or affiliated organizations. But to what extent are these theories credible? Is there evidence that corroborate them?

These questions seem legitimate, provided that ready-made answers are not accepted without convincing evidence. However, it is difficult to get this kind of evidence, and we might need another Edward Snowden or WikiLeaks to learn the real truth about the relationship between IS and US intelligence.

Yet not having this evidence should not prevent us from trying to gather some clues that may not amount to definitive evidence, but which will no doubt question the narrative that fully exonerates US intelligence from involvement with the jihadis.

First of all, most IS leaders had passed through the former U.S. detention facility at Camp Bucca in Iraq. So who were the most prominent of these detainees?

Abu Ayman al-Iraqi... also "graduated" from Camp Bucca, and currently serves as a member on IS' military council. The leader of IS, Abu Bakr al-Baghdadi, tops the list. He was detained from 2004 until mid-2006. After he was released, he formed the Army of Sunnis, which later merged with the so-called Mujahideen Shura Council.

What happened during Baghdadi's detention in Bucca remains a mystery. Some press reports said he had been detained as a "civilian" in prison for 10 months in 2004, while other reports stated he was captured by the US forces in 2005 and held for four years at Camp Bucca. This latter possibility is unlikely, given that Baghdadi had formed the Army of Sunnis and joined the Mujahideen Shura Council shortly before the assassination of Abu Musab al-Zarqawi in June 2006. This is while bearing in mind that this council was established in January 2006, which makes it more likely that Baghdadi had been released either in late 2005 or early 2006.

It should be noted that after the Army of the Sunnis merged with the Mujahideen Shura Council, the Americans were able to successfully hunt down the leaders of al-Qaeda in Iraq, starting with Zarqawi in 2006, and not ending with Abu Omar al-Baghdadi and Abu Hamza al-Muhajir in 2010, the death of the former being the event that paved the way for Abu Bakr al-Baghdadi to become the organization's leader.

Another prominent IS leader today is Abu Ayman al-Iraqi, who was a former officer in the Iraqi army under Saddam Hussein. This man also "graduated" from Camp Bucca, and currently serves as a member on IS' military council.

Another member of the military council who was in Bucca is Adnan Ismail Najm. He was known a(Abu Abdul_Rahman al-Bilawi). IS named the operation for the "invasion of Mosul" after him. He was detained on January 2005 in Bucca, and was also a former officer in Saddam's army. He was the head of a shura council in IS, before he was killed by the Iraqi army near Mosul on June 4, 2014.

Camp Bucca was also home to Haji Samir, aka Haji Bakr, whose real name is Samir Abed Hamad al-Obeidi al-Dulaimi. He was a colonel in the army of the former Iraqi regime. He was detained in Bucca, and after his release, he joined al-Qaeda. He was the top man in ISIS in Syria, but was killed in Aleppo in the first week of January 2014.

According to the testimonies of US officers who worked in the prison, the administration of Camp Bucca had taken measures including the segregation of prisoners on the basis of their ideology. This, according to experts, made it possible to recruit people directly and indirectly. Former detainees had said in documented television interviews that Bucca, which was closed down in September 2009, was akin to an "al-Qaeda school» where senior extremist gave lessons on explosives and suicide attacks to younger prisoners. A former prisoner named Adel Jassem Mohammed said that one of the extremists remained in the prison for two weeks only, but even so was able to recruit 25 out of 34 inmates who were there. Mohammed also said that U.S. military officials did nothing to stop the extremists from mentoring the other detainees.

While Camp Bucca is the common denominator among most IS leaders, another one is the fact that a majority of them were officers in the Baathist army, which explains the ease with which the radical group has been able to infiltrate the clans and coax some of their leaders into joining its ranks.

Another noteworthy point is that none of the leaders who had emerged out of Bucca and who were subsequently killed, were killed in U.S. airstrikes, but rather at the hands of the Iraqi army, the Syrian army, or in fighting with other armed groups.

What had happened in Bucca then? What were the circumstances that made all those former detainees subsequent leaders in the extremist group? These questions require answers and serious investigations. No doubt, we will one day discover that many more leaders in the group had been detained in Bucca as well, which seems to have been more of a "terrorist academy" than a prison.

FITNA

In the years after the U.S. invasion of Afghanistan but before the invasion of Iraq, Zarqawi had not yet achieved infamy. He bounced around between Iran, Iraqi Kurdistan, Syria, and the Sunni Triangle in Iraq, gaining new jihadist contacts. Within a half year after the invasion of Iraq, however, Zarqawi became a household name for his brutal personal beheadings and fast-paced suicide bombing campaign against Shiite religious targets and Sunni civilians, among others.

As a result of these successes, many foreign fighters wanted to join, and the group needed more resources to continue and expand its operations. Further, not to be outdone by Zarqawi, bin Laden himself wanted to "own" the Iraq jihad as well as remain relevant while hiding from the United States. Given these dynamics, in the October 2004 issue of Muaskar al-Batar (The Sword Training Camp),12 Zarqawi relented to bin Laden, pledging baya to him and renaming his group *al-Qaeda in the Land of Two Rivers* after eight months of negotiations.

In Iraq, and now part of the al-Qaeda network, Zarqawi's group controlled resources and the flow of foreign fighters, helping it gain loyalty from individual fighters. This is important because AQI thus controlled many of the informal networks and the future generation of the jihadist movement. One of the key factors now separating ISIS from al-Qaeda relates to this generational difference.

In April 2013, overt enmity between ISIS and al-Qaeda broke out in full when ISIS leader Abu Bakr al-Baghdadi announced that he was extending the Islamic State of Iraq into Syria and changing the group's name to the Islamic State of Iraq and al-Sham. He also noted an open secret that ISIS and JN were one and the same. This did not sit well with JN leader Abu Muhammadal-Jawlani, who rebuoed the move into Syria and reaffirmed his allegiance to Zawahiri. In turn, Zawahiri later tried, but failed, to nullify Baghdadi's power play by telling ISIS to return to the Iraq front and leave the Syrian front to JN.

Neither Jawlani nor Zawahiri was allegedly consulted in advance about the expansion of the Islamic state. Baghdadi released an audio message stating ISIS would remain in Syria and would not adhere to a division based on the Sykes-Picot deal dating to World War I.

Moreover Baghdadi also gave Zawahiri al-Qaeda's most "brazen" rebuke from an affiliate ever, stating in the same audio message that Baghdadi had *"chosen the command of my Lord over the command in the letter that contradicts it."* Therefore, contrary to the original media narrative that JN had merged with ISIS, the two groups actually separated.

The context for the recent split can be found in late summer 2011, when ISI began the first stages of its comeback because of the Syrian uprising. Baghdadi dispatched operatives to Syria to set up a new jihadist organization, which Zawahiri was involved in planning, too. Among the operatives was Jawlani, whose group, JN, publicly announced itself in late January 2012.

By November 2012, Jawlani had built JN into one of the opposition's best fighting forces and locals viewed its members as fair arbiters when addressing corruption and providing social services. Such success helped inspire Baghdadi to extend his group's writ into Syria. Syrians, he felt, got to know JN members on their own terms rather than being falsely guided by media "misrepresentations" and therefore felt it opportune to announce the expansion.

At first, it appeared the JN-ISIS feud would be settled behind the scenes. Publicly, both ISIS and JN tried to put a good face on the matter, suggesting that a battle - field competition against a common foe, the Assad regime, would benefit everyone. Al-Qaeda also enlisted emissaries as mediators, among them Abu Khalid al-Suri, a now deceased senior leader in Ahrar al-Sham—a more locally focused Salafi rebel group in Syria—and Sheikh Abu Sulayman al-Muhajir, an Australian who serves as one of JN's top sharia officials. None of these negotiations yielded success. Al-Qaeda's ultimate disaffiliation with ISIS occurred as a result of various factors, including the January 2014 uprising against ISIS by main-stream Syrian rebels over the group's excesses; the group's general predatory way of taking territory and resources from other rebel groups; and a failed public reconciliation effort by the independent Saudi cleric Abd Allah bin Muhammad al-Muhaysini—along-side the failed private attempts mentioned earlier.

On February 2, 2014, al-Qaeda's general command (AQGC) released a statement that said: ISIS is not a branch of the Qaidat al-Jihad group, we have no organizational relationship with it, and the group is not responsible for its actions.

Afterward, Adnani went after Zawahiri by responding, If God decrees to you [Zawahiri] to set foot in the land of the Islamic state, he should pledge allegiance to it and be a soldier of its amir [Baghdadi]. AQGC's statement began what both ISIS and al-Qaeda/JN describe as a fitna (state of discord), which has led to open warfare in Syria that continues to this day.

In addition to killing one another on the battle-field, including Abu Khalid al-Suri, both groups have used media to lure fence-sitters and possible defectors among the global jihadist community. It is likely that social media, especially Twitter, has amplified mutual hatred, with supporters of each camp refusing to back down rhetorically, likely signaling their steadfastness to their respective leaders. One wonders whether the situation would have become so hostile a decade ago, when al-Qaeda could control the message on its password-protected forums. Each group also released official testimonies from defectors from the other side. A JN video series from ISIS defectors is called "Muhajirinunder Siege."

A nine-part ISIS video series, "Series of the Life from the Words of the Ulama [religious scholars] on the Project of the Islamic State," high-lights positive comments about the creation of its Islamic state from its own past leaders (Zarqawi, Abu Hamza al-Muhajir, and Abu Omar al-Baghdadi), al-Qaeda leaders (bin Laden and Abu Yahya al-Libi), and a leader of al-Qaeda in the Arabian Peninsula, or AQAP (Anwar al-Awlaqi). The main argument between ISIS and al-Qaeda/JN is over authority and methodology (manhaj) as well as revisionist history. ISIS views Zawahiri's authority as illegitimate, even if prior sentiments noted earlier would suggest otherwise, and his organization as having deviated from the path of bin Laden. ISIS considers itself the true heir of bin Laden's al-Qaeda,but under the new banner of the Islamic state.

For example, in early April 2014, Adnani claimed that the leaders of al-Qaeda deviated from the right manhaj, we say this as sadness overwhelms us and bit-terness fills our hearts...Verily al-Qaeda today has ceased to be the base of jihad, rather its leadership has become an axe supporting the destruction of the project of the Islamic State and the coming khilafa (caliphate)...al-Qaeda now runs after the bandwagon of the majority and calls them as 'the Umma,' and softens in their stance at the expense of the religion, and the taghut (tyrants) of the Ikhwan (Muslim Brotherhood).

For their part, al-Qaeda and Zawahiri claim that Baghdadi did, in fact, pledge baya to Zawahiri, though privately. Therefore, according to this rea-soning, Baghdadi and ISIS broke a religious oath and have become a deviant group that disobeyed the emir's orders, specifically relating to its failure to carry out jihad in its designated location, Iraq.

Beyond the more technical arguments between leaders in these organizations, ISIS and JN have also acted differently on the ground in Syria. For ISIS, which believes it truly is an Islamic state, all residents of territory it takes over fall under the group's sovereign will and must abide by its interpretations of God's law. In this model, no competition or power sharing can be acceptable. It is true that ISIS has added a "hearts and minds" component to its governing strategy, but it has kept its narrower interpretations of sharia pertaining to social or criminal issues.

In contrast, JN views itself as one among many groups (primarily other Islamist allies) that must work together not only to fight against the Assad regime, but also to govern liberated spaces.

JN takes the long view that it cannot force its ideas on individuals and therefore must pursue a more gradualist approach, based on the lessons of past failed attempts at jihadist governance in Iraq last decade, as well as Somalia, Yemen, and Mali. The key is to socialize and normalize its ideas over time so that eventually the group can legitimately implement its more narrow interpretations of sharia. While this approach may have greater appeal for locals, ISIS's "forcing it down people's throats" style is more popular with its foreign fighter contingent, which makes up about 50 percent of its fighting force and provides support for its out-of-theater power projection.

While the fight between ISIS and al-Qaeda/JN has mainly played out within the Syrian zone of conflict, it has affected jihadist organizations and factions in other locales. For instance, while both AQAP and al-Qaeda in the Islamic Maghreb (AQIM) have kept a neutral position and called for reconciliation between the two groups, AQIM's central region came out in support of ISIS in late March 2014.5 The central region's legitimacy, however, has been questioned considering that the signers of its statement were previously unknown.

Additionally, in late January 2014, some AQAP fighters in Syria have in their own capacity backed ISIS, including as expressed by the AQAP leader Hatim al-Mamun. Closer to home, a breakaway faction of nine individuals in al-Qaeda in Afghanistan, including Maqdisi's brother and some other relevant leaders, pledged baya to Baghdadi in early April 2014.

This forced one of al-Qaeda's ideologues, Abu Amir al-Naji, to respond in late May 2014 that the nine-person letter made false claims against al-Qaeda. Such a response to the defection of just nine people illustrates al-Qaeda's worries about its ability to win the war of ideas with the future generation of global jihadists. In addition, other regional groups like Ansar al-Sharia in both Tunisia and Libya as well as jihadists in Gaza/Sinai and Indonesia have posted pro-ISIS propaganda.

All has not been lost for al-Qaeda, however. In late April 2014 Mokhtar Belmokhtar, the emir of the group al-Murabitun—an al-Qaeda branch in the greater Sahara—backed Zawahiri and al-Qaeda: It is incumbent upon us to confirm our confidence and commitment to the manhaj and guidance of our emir, Shaykh Ayman al-Zawahiri, out of our faith in the correctness of this manhaj, which is built upon perception and correct jurisprudence, and steady, successful, and blessed steps.

Additionally, in mid-May 2014, the emir of Harakat Shabab al-Mujahedin in Somalia, Sheikh Mukhtar Abu al-Zubair, confirmed support for Zawahiri's efforts in dealing with ISIS. Zubair also specifically endorsed Zawahiri's November 2012 release, "The Treatise of Supporting Islam," which highlights the importance of implementing sharia and liberating occupied Muslim lands.

Even more recently, Ali Abu Muhammad, the leader of the Caucasus Emirate (CE), a jihadist group that is not a branch of al-Qaeda, expressed sympathy for JN's side. This is likely because the CE's branch in Syria, Jaish al-Muhajireen wal Ansar, is close with JN. These three overt endorsements are unlikely to tip the scales toward al-Qaeda, but it does provide reassurances in addition to the support from JN, AQAP, and AQIM. It also highlights that al-Qaeda is not defeated.

Al-Qaeda is having a difficult time, given ISIS battlefield gains in both Syria and Iraq. Continued success for ISIS, of course, is by no means guaranteed, especially given the group's tendency to overplay its hand with locals. But unlike in Iraq a decade ago, there is no force like the United States on the ground to consolidate insurgent gains against ISIS. As seen in Syria since January, many nationalists, mainstream Islamists, and even JN have been unable to strategically defeat ISIS. And now that ISIS has gained new resources in the recent Iraq battles, it is pouring them into new offenses and regaining lost territory. Further, the reality of a proto-state and ISIS's willingness to try to govern—this khilafa project, as many within the group call it—is quite appealing to jihadists. ISIS is not only talking the talk about establishing an Islamic state, it is walking the walk. This has attracted many foreign fighters to its side.

In becoming the beacon for foreign fighters over the past year, ISIS now controls many recruitment and facilitation/logistics networks. Further, those who have fought with ISIS have made connections with one another and will likely keep in touch when they return to their places of origin. The solidarity and brotherhood established through fighting on the front lines and enduring the same hardships cements these relationships, which will be important for the future of the jihadist movement. Additionally, individuals like winners and, unlike al-Qaeda, which has not had a clear victory in a decade, ISIS continues to build its prestige and legitimacy within the overall movement.

The composition of foreign fighter sent to Syria (and now to Iraq again) indicates that the movement's future is being decided by Saudis, Libyans, Tunisians, and Jordanians. In terms of the Saudis, one question to be answered is whether returnees to AQAP can execute a coup against AQAP's leadership. AQAP remains loyal to Zawahiri given its emir Nasir al-Wihayshi's relations with bin Laden, which go back to Afghanistan. That said, if Wihayshi is killed in an American drone strike, anything could happen. AQAP, still viewed as al-Qaeda's strongest branch, is a bellwether and if it leans toward ISIS in the near to medium future, ISIS will have won the war against al-Qaeda. Similarly, with ISIS's victories next door in Iraq, members of JN may have more cause to defect back to ISIS, which could be a fatal blow to al-Qaeda as well. There are already small signs of such movement, especially in Deir al-Zour and Damascus.

Looking to North Africa, where a third safe haven exists outside the Syria/Iraq and Yemen arenas, many of the Tunisians and Libyans who fought in ISIS were originally members of Ansar al-Sharia in Tunisia (AST) and Ansar al-Sharia in Libya (ASL), which could help make both groups kingpins in the Maghrebi landscape, especially since they continue to grow closer organizationally themselves.65 Addition-ally, the Darnah-based jihadist group Majlis Shura Shabab al-Islam publicly voiced support for ISIS earlier this week.

Unlike the Saudis, Libyans, and Tunisians, the Jordanians are still more sympathetic to JN than to ISIS, which could hurt the latter's ability to project further into the Levant. Lastly, in terms of Westerners, most of whom come from European Union countries (three thousand–plus), most are now with ISIS. Any plots or attacks in the West will thus more likely emanate from ISIS than from al-Qaeda. Various possibilities could either help or hinder the prospects of ISIS or al-Qaeda.

For ISIS, major local backlash or deaths in the leadership could do harm. For al-Qaeda, drone strikes against the leadership in Pakistan or AQAP's leaders in Yemen could potentially accelerate ISIS's claim over the global jihadist movement. There are even rumors that there could be a Ramadan reconciliation between the two in the coming weeks, which would likely beet ISIS, since it has more of the leverage over al-Qaeda in light of the recent Iraq offensives. It is impossible to of course predict the future since for example many in 2006 viewed Zarqawi and AQI as permanently eclipsing al-Qaeda, yet this did not end up happening.

If al-Qaeda wants to reclaim some semblance of legitimacy, it will desperately pursue a major strike along the lines of the Madrid train bombings, the July 7, 2005, London attacks, or actualizing the failed AQAP plots in 2009 and 2010. At this point, though, momentum toward ISIS may be too great for both the short and the longer term. Will the U.S. withdrawal from Afghanistan help resuscitate an organization that has taken many leadership hits in the past few years? It is too early to know, but if current trends hold, ISIS has opened up a lead on al-Qaeda, which has a steep hill to climb just to stave off its own relative decline...

Syrian Jihad

In an unexpected and unprecedented turn of events, al-Qaeda members and jihadists from all over the world who embrace the ideology of global jihad are now doubting the group's leader, Ayman al-Zawahiri, and calling for his removal.

While the Syrian Jihad has been of paramount concern to world governments, with hundreds of foreign fighters pouring in to participate in the fighting, the country has also been an arena for internal strife and bloody battles between the al-Qaeda-affiliated al-Nusra Front and al-Qaeda's former branch, the Islamic State in Iraq and the Levant (ISIL). Members of al-Qaeda and jihadists together blame Zawahiri for mismanaging the conflict in Syria and enflaming sedition, and advocate new leadership.

Under Zawahiri's command, al-Qaeda assigned the al-Nusra Front to be its arm in Syria, and disavowed the ISIL, telling jihadists that it does not acknowledge its founding and rejects its activities. Shortly after al-Qaeda clearly delineated its position, on February 23, 2014, Zawahiri's representative in Syria, Abu Khalid al-Suri, was killed in a suicide bombing in Aleppo. This was the watershed moment for the conflict. The al-Nusra Front and their supporters accused the ISIL of perpetrating the act and demanded they submit to arbitration by an independent Shariah body, while the ISIL denied having any connection.

Representing al-Qaeda's core leadership, Adam Gadahn (AKA Azzam the American) spoke first on the issue, noting that jihadi factions in Syria blamed a "group that is known for its extreme nature and radical behavior," which infuriated pro-ISIL supporters, believing that Gadahn was referring to the ISIL.

After Zawahiri made a similar accusation in a speech released on April 4, 2014, those same jihadists quickly attacked him, questioning his wisdom and demanding his removal. While the entire situation is unprecedented in the contemporary jihad, it is unfathomable that jihadists not only express such vitriol towards the leader of al-Qaeda, but on an al-Qaeda-affiliated password-protected forums, the house for al-Qaeda for a decade, to brand him a disbeliever and seek a replacement. The assault on Zawahiri became so fierce, that administrators of the top-tier jihadi forum Shumukh al-Islam deleted all the posts in the discussion thread for the speech, "Eulogy for the Martyr of Sedition Abu Khalid al-Suri," and locked it. A few hours later, the forum went down for "maintenance".

As some jihadists cursed Zawahiri and others questioned his authority, in a separate discussion, a Shumukh al-Islam user, "Ta'ir al-Nawras," representing the views of the many members who were angered by Zawahiri's message, demanded that Zawahiri be stripped of his leadership position and that it be given to al-Qaeda in the Arabian Peninsula (AQAP) chief Abu Baseer Nasser al-Wuhayshi.

Sheikh Abu Baseer is closer to the course of events in the Islamic world, and he is wiser, more cunning, and more capable to deal with it. He was one of the assistants of Sheikh Usama, may Allah have mercy on him, he was enabled to restructure the al-Qaeda branch in the Arabian Peninsula. He strengthened it, and made it a difficult number, and one of the most powerful branches of the organization in the world, superior even to the Central Command. The branch of the organization was enabled under his leadership to reach the United States of America with several operations, among which was the invasion of Umar al-Farouk, may Allah release him.

Also, the command of al-Qaeda in the Arabian Peninsula is stronger and has better capabilities, and the experiences of its leaders are better, and the efficiency of its personnel is higher.

Still, there are some jihadists who hope to calm the situation and restore order. One forum user, "Nasa'im al-Kheir," illustrates the views from the other side, explained that while Zawahiri made "mistakes" in his handling of the Syrian conflict, it does not allow Muslims to attack him and brand him a "disbeliever". He wrote:

Although we disagree with the Sheikh, may Allah the Almighty preserve him, on the issue of al-Sham [Syria] and what happened in it, and it is a huge dispute, it does not contest the religion of the Sheikh and the authenticity of his method. Who are we to question the religion of the Sheikh, let alone speak of his mistakes and imperfections?

Similar to "Ta'ir al-Nawras" in his post, "Nasa'im al-Kheir" also pointed out Zawahiri's isolation in the Afghanistan-Pakistan area, far away from Syria, as a reason for his faulty judgment:

The mistakes of the Sheikh are mistakes that happen with any commander, and we still excuse him (if we excuse he who fell into the disbelief by ignorance). So it is the foremost excuse for the Sheikh that he is away from the reality in al-Sham and the truth is absent from him.

As the conflict rages and jihadists further entrench themselves in separate camps, al-Qaeda will remain marginalized in Syria until it is able to broker a solution. The sedition has impacted the jihadists and al-Qaeda on many fronts: from the disputes on the jihadi forums and social media to as far as the battlefield, with the ongoing bloody fights between the two sides.

The jihadi generation raised on the unquestionable leadership of Usama bin Laden, the fiery speeches of Abu Musab al-Zarqawi, and the brazen actions of al-Qaeda's branch in Iraq for nearly a decade is finding it difficult to accept a leader who is far from the battlefield in question and unable to exercise authority or connect with his followers. Pro-ISIL jihadists view the group as holding the birthright of al-Qaeda in Iraq, and not the al-Nusra Front, and accept its positions as truth and those who oppose them as the enemy, including Ayman al-Zawahiri and Adam Gadahn.

www.ingramcontent.com/pod-product-compliance
Lightning Source LLC
Chambersburg PA
CBHW081158280526
45787CB00008B/3375